PATHWAY TO RENEWAL (P2R)
A 26-Week Recovery & Stabilization Guide to Healing, Stability & Growth

By Kerry L. Shipman, Ph.D., J.D., MPA, CADC

The Ship Group Services LLC.

www.Pathway2Renewal.org

© 2025 by Dr. Kerry L. Shipman

All rights reserved.

No part of this publication may be reproduced, distributed, or transmitted in any form or by any means, including photocopying, recording, or other electronic or mechanical methods, without the prior written permission of the author or publisher, except in the case of brief quotations embodied in critical reviews and certain other noncommercial uses permitted by copyright law.

For inquiries, contact:

The Ship Group Services LLC.

3126 Milton Road, Suite 215

Charlotte, NC 28215

ISBN: 979-8-218-70126-0

Printed in the United States of America

Program Introduction & Overview
Welcome to the Pathway to Renewal (P2R) Program

You made it. And that means something. Whether you're starting over or just trying again, this is a chance to build something solid. This workbook—and the team behind it—is here to walk with you as you take back your time, your power, and your peace.

The **Pathway to Renewal (P2R)** program was created for people who've been through real-life struggles—homelessness, incarceration, addiction, trauma, or mental health challenges—and are now ready to move forward. This isn't a quick fix. It's a process. One step at a time. One page at a time.

This workbook is your personal space. Use it to track your progress, stay grounded, and remind yourself of what you're working toward. It's here to support what you're already doing with your therapist, peer support specialist, case manager, or reentry coach.

What You'll Gain

Over the next 26 weeks, you'll work with your support team to:

- Build a stable foundation for housing and employment
- Set goals that matter—and actually follow through
- Learn how to manage stress, triggers, and emotions
- Take ownership of your time, money, and choices
- Strengthen your support system
- Reflect on your growth and finish with purpose

This isn't just about surviving—it's about rebuilding a life you can be proud of.

What Makes This Program Different

You won't find fake hype or sugarcoated success stories here. This was created by someone who's lived through struggle—and got up anyway. This program is **real**, **direct**, and **made for people like you**.

We know life isn't perfect. You might miss days. You might get off track. That's okay. The goal is to stay in it and keep moving forward.

What You Can Expect from Us

As a participant in the P2R program, you'll receive:

- A dedicated support person to walk with you through this journey
- Help with housing, employment, and life goals
- Weekly check-ins to track progress and plan next steps
- Emotional and mental health support
- Respect, dignity, and confidentiality at every step

What We Ask of You

To get the most out of this program, we ask that you:

- **Stay committed** – Show up and do your best, even when it's tough
- **Be real with us** – Let us know when you're struggling
- **Keep trying** – Even if you fall off, get back up
- **Be respectful** – Of your support team, other participants, and yourself
- **Follow through** – On goals, assignments, and communication

Mental Health Is Part of the Plan

We don't treat mental health like an afterthought. If your mind's not right, it's hard to move forward. That's why this workbook includes:

- Mental health check-ins and reflection questions
- Crisis & Safety Planning
- Tools for stress, triggers, and emotional regulation
- Space to talk about what's real—without judgment

Using This Workbook

This workbook is a support tool—not a test or assignment. You can:

- Use it with your therapist, peer support, or case manager
- Complete as much or as little as you need each week
- Keep it private or share with your support team
- Use it during sessions, workshops, or on your own time

Your Rights

You have the right to:

- Be treated with dignity and respect
- Participate in planning your goals
- Accept or decline services
- Ask questions and get clear answers
- File a complaint or grievance without fear
- Have your information kept private under HIPAA and state law
- Be safe—physically, mentally, and emotionally
- Speak for yourself and define your own success

My Right to Choose

I understand that I have the right to:

- Set personal goals and define success in my own terms
- Choose which services I receive and participate in planning
- Decide which natural supports (family/friends) are involved in my care
- Decline any service or intervention that makes me feel unsafe

I also acknowledge that I have been informed of my right to access 24/7 crisis support.

Provider's 24/7 Crisis Hotline

Provider Agency Name:

_____

Provider's Phone 24/7 Phone Line

_____

Mobile Crisis (Local Provider):

_____

NC 988 Suicide & Crisis Lifeline:

Dial 988

Final Word Before You Start

You've been through enough. This isn't just a workbook—it's your reset. This is your proof that you haven't given up. And we're not giving up on you either.

You still deserve peace. You still have purpose. Let's get to work.

2025 Pathway to Renewal (P2R) | www.Pathway2Renewal.org | All rights reserved.

Table of Contents

Introduction

- Welcome to P2R
- How This Workbook Works
- What Makes This Different
- Your Starting Point: Self-Assessment

Phase 1: Stabilization & Reflection

- Week 1 – Ground Zero: Where Are You Now?
- Week 2 – What Got You Here?
- Week 3 – Mindset, Triggers & Temptation
- Week 4 – Replacing Old Habits
- Week 5 – Establishing Routine & Structure

Phase 2: Taking Control

- Week 6 – Understanding Trauma
- Week 7 – Relationships & Communication
- Week 8 – Conflict, Control & Choices
- Week 9 – Housing & Stability
- Week 10 – Employment & Readiness
- Week 11 – Budgeting & Financial Basics
- Week 12 – Staying Sober, Staying Focused

Phase 3: Rebuilding Your Life

- Week 13 – Healthy Support Systems
- Week 14 – Long-Term Goals & Vision
- Week 15 – Giving Back: Service & Legacy
- Week 16 – Triggers Revisited: What's Changed?
- Week 17 – Re-entry & Community Connection
- Week 18 – Self-Care, Health & Wellness
- Week 19 – Boundaries & Respect
- Week 20 – Time Management
- Week 21 – Redefining Success
- Week 22 – Employment: Leveling Up
- Week 23 – Sustaining Change
- Week 24 – Preparing for What's Next
- Week 25 – Final Self-Assessment
- Week 26 – Graduation Reflection

Appendix & Resources

- Resource List & Notes
- Certificate of Completion

A Personal Message from Dr. Kerry L. Shipman

Dear Participant,

Welcome to the Pathway to Renewal Program. My name is **Dr. Kerry L. Shipman**, and I want you to know something right from the start: **I believe in you.** I created this program because I've seen what it's like when people are trying to rebuild their lives but don't have the right support. I've worked with people coming out of tough situations—whether it's homelessness, the justice system, addiction, or just feeling stuck—and I've watched them fight for a second chance.

I've also faced my own challenges in life. I know what it's like to be counted out, to struggle, and to feel like you're starting over. That's why this program isn't just paperwork or tasks—it's a step-by-step guide to help you build something solid for yourself, with real tools and support along the way.

You don't have to do this alone. Your program provider is here to walk with you, help you complete each part, and make sure you're moving toward your goals. Every page in this workbook is a step forward. Some steps will feel small, but they all matter.

I want you to know that I didn't create this program to check a box. I created it because

I care about what happens to you.

I want you to win.

I want you to finish.

> I want you to be able to look back and say, "I did that."

I'm proud of you for being here. Let's take it one step at a time—**and don't stop until you're where you want to be.**

Sincerely,

[signature]

Dr. Kerry Shipman, J.D, MPA. CADC
Founder, Pathway to Renewal (P2R)
Executive Director, TSG Behavioral Health & Community Services

Getting Started

Before we begin, let's set a strong foundation for your journey.

Personal Information

(Fill in the blanks)

Full Name: _____

Date of Birth: _____

Contact Number: _____

Assigned Program: _____

Assigned Program Provider: _____

Provider Contact Information: _____

2025 Pathway to Renewal (P2R) | www.Pathway2Renewal.org | All rights reserved.

COMMITMENT AGREEMENT

Your Commitment to <u>Yourself</u>

I don't know what you've been through.
Maybe you've slept outside.
Maybe you've been locked up.
Maybe you've lost everything.
Maybe you've done things you're not proud of.
Maybe you feel like nobody believes in you anymore.

But I want you to know this: **you're still here.**
And as long as you're here, you've still got a chance.

This program won't fix everything overnight.
You're going to have hard days.
You're going to want to give up.
You might fall back.
You might not feel like talking to us.
You might even hate showing up.

But I'm asking you—**don't quit.**
Don't quit on yourself.
Don't quit on this chance.
Don't quit on the life you still have left.

By signing this, you're not saying you'll be perfect.
You're saying you'll keep fighting.
You'll keep showing up.
You'll keep trying, even if it's messy.

You're saying you'll let us walk beside you, even when it's hard.

Because no matter where you're starting from—**you deserve to get up.**
You deserve to heal.
You deserve a future.

And I want to see you win.

Participant Signature: _____ Date: _____

Program Provider Signature: _____ Date: _____

Graduation Summary & Discharge Planning

At the end of this program, I will complete a final reflection and exit plan. These are the key outcomes I hope to achieve before discharge:

- ☑ Stable housing
- ☑ Income or job readiness
- ☑ Continued therapy or recovery supports
- ☑ Support network in place
- ☑ Crisis plan updated
- ☑ Skills/tools for independence

Setting Your Goals

Think about other personal goals I want to accomplish in this program.

My 3 biggest goals in the next six months are:

1. _____
2. _____
3. _____

Three small steps I can take to reach my goals are:

1. _____
2. _____
3. _____

2025 Pathway to Renewal (P2R) | www.Pathway2Renewal.org | All rights reserved.

Self-Check: Where Am I Right Now?

Take a moment to rate how you're feeling as you begin this program. You'll check back at the end to see how far you've come.

Area of Life	Not Confident	Somewhat Confident	Very Confident
I have stable housing	☐	☐	☐
I can find and keep a job	☐	☐	☐
I manage my stress well	☐	☐	☐
I have healthy support around me	☐	☐	☐
I have a plan for my future	☐	☐	☐
I know what to do in a crisis	☐	☐	☐
I believe I can finish this program	☐	☐	☐

Today's Date: _____

You'll fill this out again during your graduation week (Week 26) to see how much has changed.

Mental Health & Well-Being

Check in with yourself regularly. Circle how you feel today:

 Happy

 Neutral

 Stressed

 Sad

 Angry

 Tired

List three things you are grateful for today:

➤ _____
➤ _____
➤ _____

Phase 1: Immediate Stabilization (Weeks 1-4)

Goal: Ensure basic needs are met, establish structure, and build a foundation for success.

Week 1: Orientation & Needs Assessment

Daily Tasks:

- Attend program orientation and meet your assigned provider.
- Complete the **pre-evaluation form** to assess immediate needs.
- Identify urgent concerns such as housing, food security, and employment barriers.
- Develop a structured **daily routine**.
- Begin **mental health & substance use assessments**, if applicable.

Participant Assignments:

- Write a **commitment to self-letter**, describing what you hope to achieve.
- Gather and organize **personal documents** (ID, Social Security card, medical records).
- Create a **daily routine planner**.

Commitment to Self-Letter

Write a letter to yourself, committing to this program and your personal growth. What do you hope to achieve? What changes do you want to make in your life?

Dear Future Me,

I am starting this journey because
_____
_____
_____
_____.

My biggest hope for myself is
_____
_____
_____
_____.

When I face challenges, I will remind myself that
_____
_____
_____
_____.

By the end of this program, I want to
_____
_____
_____
_____.

Signed,

_____.
(Your Name)

Weekly Reflection Journal – Week 1

You made it through Week 1. That's something. A lot of people don't even show up. This is your space to be real—no judgment. Just be honest about where you're starting.

This week, I made progress in:

_____
_____
_____

One challenge I faced was:

_____
_____
_____

Something I learned about myself was:

_____
_____
_____

My goal for next week is:

_____
_____
_____

Reflection Prompt: What do I hope this program will help me become?

_____
_____
_____

Week 2: Public Benefits & Employment Readiness

Daily Tasks:

- Apply for **Medicaid, SNAP, and rental assistance**.
- Complete a **job readiness assessment**.
- Identify **employment barriers** (criminal record, skill gaps, transportation issues).

Participant Assignments:

- Research **three potential jobs** that match skills or interest.
- Complete a **strengths & weaknesses worksheet**.

Job Readiness Assessment Worksheet

Employment History

1. **Have you ever been employed?** ☐ Yes ☐ No
   o If yes, list your last three jobs:

   Employer Job Title Start Date End Date Reason for Leaving

2. **What type of work are you interested in?** _____
3. **Do you have any certifications, licenses, or special skills?** ☐ Yes ☐ No
   o If yes, please list them: _____

Identifying Employment Barriers

4. **What challenges have prevented you from obtaining or keeping a job?** (Check all that apply) ☐ Lack of experience
   ☐ No transportation
   ☐ Criminal record
   ☐ Disability/health concerns
   ☐ Lack of childcare
   ☐ Housing instability
   ☐ Substance use
   ☐ Lack of job search skills
   ☐ Other (please specify): _____
5. **How do you currently get around for work, appointments, or errands?** ☐ Personal vehicle
   ☐ Public transportation
   ☐ Rides from family/friends
   ☐ Walking/Biking
   ☐ No transportation available
6. **What steps are you willing to take to overcome these barriers?**
   o _____
   o _____

Job Search Readiness

7. **Do you have a current resume?** ☐ Yes ☐ No
8. **Do you know how to apply for jobs online?** ☐ Yes ☐ No

9. **Do you have access to a computer or internet for job searching?** ☐ Yes ☐ No
10. **What industries are you open to working in?** (Check all that apply) ☐ Retail
    ☐ Customer service
    ☐ Food service
    ☐ Construction/Labor
    ☐ Office/Admin
    ☐ Healthcare
    ☐ Other: _____

Interview Preparation

11. **Do you feel comfortable in job interviews?** ☐ Yes ☐ No
12. **What areas do you need help with?** (Check all that apply) ☐ Answering common interview questions
    ☐ Talking about my skills
    ☐ Handling nervousness
    ☐ Dressing professionally
    ☐ Other: _____
13. **Do you own professional clothing for interviews?** ☐ Yes ☐ No
14. **Would you like help with mock interviews?** ☐ Yes ☐ No

Next Steps & Goal Setting

15. **What are your top three employment goals?**

    - _____
    - _____
    - _____

16. **What steps can you take this week to move closer to employment?**

    - _____
    - _____

17. **Would you like assistance with:** (Check all that apply) ☐ Resume writing
    ☐ Job search support
    ☐ Interview coaching
    ☐ Workplace readiness training
    ☐ Other: _____

Weekly Reflection Journal – Week 2

It's easy to get discouraged when it feels like you're starting over. But don't forget: you showed up again. Take a minute to think about what moved you forward this week.

This week, I made progress in:

_____
_____
_____

One challenge I faced was:

_____
_____
_____

Something I learned about myself was:

_____
_____
_____

My goal for next week is:

_____
_____
_____

Reflection Prompt: How does having a job or income change how I see myself?

_____
_____
_____

Week 3: Resume Building & Housing Preparation

Daily Tasks:

- Update or create a **resume**.
- Learn how to **search and apply for jobs online**.
- Identify **short-term and long-term housing goals**.

Participant Assignments:

- Apply for **at least one job per day**.
- Research **three potential housing options**.

Weekly Reflection Journal – Week 3

You might not be where you want to be yet, but you're not where you used to be. Think about one area of your life that felt a little more stable this week.

This week, I made progress in:

_____
_____
_____

One challenge I faced was:

_____
_____
_____

Something I learned about myself was:

_____
_____
_____

My goal for next week is:

_____
_____
_____

Reflection Prompt: How would stable housing change my day-to-day life?

_____
_____
_____

Week 4: Interview Skills & Housing Applications

Daily Tasks:

- Practice **mock interviews**.
- Begin **housing application process**.
- Conduct **wellness check-ins**.

Participant Assignments:

- Practice **answering common interview questions**.
- Fill out **at least one rental application**.

Weekly Reflection Journal – Week 4

Some parts of this will feel uncomfortable. That's okay. Growth usually does. Take a second to be proud that you're still here, still trying.

This week, I made progress in:

_____
_____
_____

One challenge I faced was:

_____
_____
_____

Something I learned about myself was:

_____
_____
_____

My goal for next week is:

_____
_____
_____

Reflection Prompt: What's one thing I can say with confidence in an interview?

_____
_____
_____

Phase 2: Building Stability (Weeks 5-8)

Goal: Strengthen job readiness, increase financial literacy, and progress toward stable housing.

Week 5: Job Search & Budgeting

- Apply for **at least five jobs**.
- Create a **budget worksheet**.

Budget Planning Worksheet

Use this worksheet to plan and track your monthly income and expenses.
Be honest about where your money goes, and use this to build habits that support your financial goals.

Section 1: Monthly Income

List all sources of income you expect each month.

Income Source	Amount ($)

Total Monthly Income: _____

Monthly Expenses

List your regular monthly expenses below.

Expense Category	Amount ($)
Rent / Housing	
Utilities	
Groceries	
Transportation	
Phone / Internet	
Medical / Health	
Debt Payments	
Savings	
Childcare	
Entertainment	
Other	

Total Monthly Expenses: _____

Section 3: Monthly Summary

Total Monthly Income: $ _____
Total Monthly Expenses: $ _____
Remaining Balance (Income - Expenses): $ _____

Reflection

What changes can you make to improve your financial situation?

_____
_____

Mental Health & Well-Being

Check in with yourself regularly. Circle how you feel today:

 Happy

 Neutral

 Stressed

 Sad

 Angry

 Tired

List three things you are grateful for today:

➢ _____
➢ _____
➢ _____

Weekly Reflection Journal – Week 5

Budgeting, planning, working—it's not always fun, but it's part of building something solid. Reflect on what you're learning about responsibility this week.

This week, I made progress in:

_____
_____
_____

One challenge I faced was:

_____
_____
_____

Something I learned about myself was:

_____
_____
_____

My goal for next week is:

_____
_____
_____

Reflection Prompt: What's the hardest part about budgeting—and what's one step I can take?

_____
_____
_____

Week 6: Housing Assistance & Communication Skills

- Apply for **housing programs**.
- Complete a **communication & boundaries worksheet**.

Communication & Boundaries Worksheet

This worksheet will help you recognize how you communicate, how others treat you, and how to set boundaries that protect your peace and progress.

Part 1: How Do You Communicate?

Check the boxes that describe your usual way of communicating:

- ☐ I speak up when something bothers me
- ☐ I stay quiet to avoid conflict
- ☐ I express myself clearly and calmly
- ☐ I shut down when I'm frustrated
- ☐ I raise my voice or get aggressive when upset
- ☐ I try to listen, but I interrupt sometimes
- ☐ I avoid difficult conversations
- ☐ I ask questions and try to understand others

What communication habits would you like to improve?

_____
_____
_____

Part 2: Setting Healthy Boundaries

Boundaries are limits you set to protect your time, energy, and well-being.
They help you stay focused and safe.

Circle any areas where you need stronger boundaries:

- Family
- Friends
- Romantic relationships
- Social media
- Work
- Roommates or housemates
- Personal time
- Saying "no" without guilt

What's one situation where your boundaries have been disrespected?

How did you respond? Would you handle it differently now?

_____
_____

Part 3: Practice the Script

Use this sentence starter when you need to set a boundary:

"I respect you, but I need _____ in order to feel safe / focused / respected."

Example:

"I respect you, but I need space to focus on my recovery right now."

Write your own:

_____
_____

Final Reflection

Why are healthy boundaries important for your success in this program and in life?

_____
_____
_____

Weekly Reflection Journal – Week 6

Real talk—communication is hard, especially when people have let you down. Think about how you handled yourself this week. Did you speak up? Hold back? Why?

This week, I made progress in:

_____
_____
_____

One challenge I faced was:

_____
_____
_____

Something I learned about myself was:

_____
_____
_____

My goal for next week is:

_____
_____
_____

Reflection Prompt: How do I handle conflict or express myself when I feel disrespected?

_____
_____
_____

Week 7: Savings & Rental Education

- Learn about **tenant rights & responsibilities**.
- Set up a **savings goal**.

Savings Plan Worksheet

Use this worksheet to set a savings goal, track your progress, and think through your habits around money. Saving is a habit—not a number. Every dollar saved is a step toward your independence.

Part 1: Set Your Savings Goal

How much money do you want to save over the next 30 days?
$_____

What are you saving for? (Check all that apply)
☐ Emergency Fund
☐ Housing Deposit
☐ Transportation (car, bus pass, Uber, etc.)
☐ Childcare or Family Needs
☐ Future Bills
☐ Something else: _____

Part 2: What Can You Save Weekly?

How much can you realistically save each week?
$_____

Where will you keep your savings?
☐ Bank account
☐ Prepaid card
☐ Cash envelope (safe place)
☐ Other: _____

Part 3: How Will You Cut Back?

List 3 things you spend money on regularly that you could reduce or pause to help you save:

1. _____
2. _____
3. _____

What's one new habit you can build to avoid overspending?

_____

Part 4: Weekly Savings Tracker

Week	Planned to Save ($)	Actually Saved ($)	Notes
Week 1			
Week 2			
Week 3			
Week 4			

Total Saved This Month: $_____

Final Reflection

What did you learn about yourself while trying to save this month?

_____
_____
_____

Weekly Reflection Journal – Week 7

Money can be a trap or a tool. It's up to you. What steps are you taking to control your money instead of it controlling you?

This week, I made progress in:

_____
_____
_____

One challenge I faced was:

_____
_____
_____

Something I learned about myself was:

_____
_____
_____

My goal for next week is:

_____
_____
_____

Reflection Prompt: What does financial independence mean to me?

_____
_____
_____

Week 8: Mental Health & Long-Term Housing Planning

- Attend **one job interview.**
- Visit **one housing property.**

Weekly Reflection Journal – Week 8

Housing stress hits different. If you're working toward stability, that's worth writing down. What does 'home' mean to you now?

This week, I made progress in:

_____
_____
_____

One challenge I faced was:

_____
_____
_____

Something I learned about myself was:

_____
_____
_____

My goal for next week is:

_____
_____
_____

Reflection Prompt: What kind of home or living situation would help me feel safe?

_____
_____
_____

Phase 3: Life Skills Development (Weeks 9-12)

Goal: Enhance time management, communication, and emotional resilience skills.

Week 9: Time Management & Goal Setting

- Learn **time management techniques** to improve productivity.
- Develop a **daily and weekly schedule**.
- Identify and set **SMART (Specific, Measurable, Achievable, Relevant, Time-bound) goals**.

Time Management & Goal Setting Worksheet

When your time has a purpose, your goals start to move. Use this worksheet to build structure into your day and focus on the things that matter most.

Part 1: How Are You Using Your Time?

Think about a typical weekday. Fill in how you usually spend your time.

Time of Day	What I'm Usually Doing
7:00 AM – 9:00 AM	
9:00 AM – 12:00 PM	
12:00 PM – 3:00 PM	
3:00 PM – 6:00 PM	
6:00 PM – 9:00 PM	
9:00 PM – 12:00 AM	

What part of your day feels the most unproductive or wasted?

_____
_____

Part 2: Daily Routine Plan

Now let's create a more structured day. Fill in how you want your schedule to look.

Time of Day	What I Want to Be Doing
7:00 AM – 9:00 AM	
9:00 AM – 12:00 PM	
12:00 PM – 3:00 PM	
3:00 PM – 6:00 PM	
6:00 PM – 9:00 PM	
9:00 PM – 12:00 AM	

Part 3: SMART Goal Setting

Pick one thing you want to achieve in the next 30 days. Make it SMART:

Specific: What exactly do I want to do?

_____

Measurable: How will I know I've done it?

_____

Achievable: Can I really do this in 30 days?

_____

Realistic: Does this match where I'm at right now?

_____

Time-bound: What's my deadline?

_____
_____

Part 4: Steps to Get It Done

What are the first 3 steps I can take this week toward this goal?

1. _____
2. _____
3. _____

Final Reflection

What usually gets in your way when you try to follow a schedule or stick to a goal?

_____

What support do you need to stay on track?

_____
_____

Mental Health & Well-Being

Check in with yourself regularly. Circle how you feel today:

● Happy

● Neutral

● Stressed

● Sad

● Angry

● Tired

List three things you are grateful for today:

➢ _____
➢ _____
➢ _____

Weekly Reflection Journal – Week 9

This week, think about how you use your time. Are you giving your energy to things that move you forward? Or just things that keep you distracted?

This week, I made progress in:

_____
_____
_____

One challenge I faced was:

_____
_____
_____

Something I learned about myself was:

_____
_____
_____

My goal for next week is:

_____
_____
_____

Reflection Prompt: What does a productive day look like for me?

_____
_____
_____

Week 10: Communication & Conflict Resolution

- Learn **active listening and conflict resolution techniques.**
- Practice **assertive communication** in different scenarios.
- Complete **a conflict resolution worksheet** to improve interpersonal skills.

Conflict Resolution Worksheet

Conflict is a part of life—but how you handle it can either build bridges or burn them. This worksheet will help you understand your reactions and give you a better way to deal with tension, arguments, or disrespect without losing your cool.

Part 1: Know Your Conflict Style

When conflict comes up, how do you usually respond? Check all that apply.

- ☐ I shut down and avoid the person
- ☐ I try to keep the peace even if I'm not okay
- ☐ I speak up calmly and try to fix it
- ☐ I get loud or aggressive when I feel disrespected
- ☐ I walk away before it gets worse
- ☐ I talk behind their back instead of addressing it
- ☐ I ask questions to understand the other side
- ☐ I threaten to cut people off when I'm upset

Part 2: Look Back to Move Forward

Think about the last time you had a real conflict. What happened?

What was the situation?

_____

How did you react?

_____

What was the outcome?

_____

If you could do it over, what would you change?

_____
_____

Part 3: Conflict Communication Script

When you're upset, it helps to have a plan. Use this template to practice a better way to speak up:

"When you _____, I felt _____. What I need is _____."

Example:

"When you didn't return my call, I felt ignored. What I need is better communication."

Write your own:

"When you _____,

I felt _____.

What I need is _____."

Part 4: Healthy Conflict Moves

Circle the ones you want to work on:

- Take a breath before I speak
- Stop cussing/yelling when angry
- Don't talk over people
- Write things down first
- Ask questions before assuming
- Walk away and come back later
- Set boundaries without disrespect
- Use "I" statements instead of blaming

Final Reflection

What would change in your life if you handled conflict better?

_____

Who can you practice healthier communication with this week?

_____

Weekly Reflection Journal – Week 10

Conflict happens—what matters is how you respond. Did you hold your own this week? Did you let something slide that you wish you hadn't?

This week, I made progress in:

_____
_____
_____

One challenge I faced was:

_____
_____
_____

Something I learned about myself was:

_____
_____
_____

My goal for next week is:

_____
_____
_____

Reflection Prompt: When I feel misunderstood, what helps me stay calm?

_____
_____
_____

Week 11: Stress Management & Self-Care

- Identify **triggers and stress management techniques.**
- Develop a **self-care plan.**
- Explore **mindfulness, relaxation, and emotional regulation strategies.**

Self-Care Plan Worksheet

Self-care isn't about spa days or expensive things. It's about protecting your peace, energy, and mindset—especially when life is hard. This plan will help you figure out what actually helps you feel better, stay focused, and avoid burnout.

Part 1: What Does Self-Care Mean to You?

When you hear the words "self-care," what do you think?

_____

What does taking care of yourself actually look like in your real life?

_____
_____

Part 2: Identify What You Need More Of

Right now, I need more of... (Check all that apply)

- ☐ Sleep or rest
- ☐ Peace and quiet
- ☐ Alone time
- ☐ Support from others
- ☐ Time outdoors
- ☐ Spiritual connection or faith
- ☐ Laughter or fun
- ☐ Better eating habits
- ☐ A sense of purpose
- ☐ Movement or exercise
- ☐ Saying "no" without guilt
- ☐ Focus on my goals

Part 3: Build Your Self-Care Routine

List 3 small things you can do this week to take care of yourself (for real):

1. _____
2. _____
3. _____

What's one boundary you can set this week to protect your peace?

Part 4: Know Your Signs

How do you know when you're burned out, overwhelmed, or not taking care of yourself?

☐ I get irritated fast
☐ I stop caring about stuff
☐ I sleep too much or not enough
☐ I feel hopeless
☐ I isolate or avoid people
☐ I spend money I don't have
☐ I relapse or fall into old habits
☐ Other: _____

Part 5: Make a Backup Plan

When I notice I'm not okay, I will...

(Choose 1 or more)

☐ Call my support person
☐ Take a break or get outside
☐ Write it down or journal
☐ Go to a meeting / talk to my therapist
☐ Re-read my goals
☐ Use my crisis or coping plan
☐ Other: _____

Final Thought

You can't pour from an empty cup. Taking care of yourself isn't selfish—it's survival. And you deserve that.

Weekly Reflection Journal – Week 11

Mental health ain't just therapy—it's checking in with yourself. How are you really feeling this week? What helped or hurt your peace?

This week, I made progress in:

_____
_____
_____

One challenge I faced was:

_____
_____
_____

Something I learned about myself was:

_____
_____
_____

My goal for next week is:

_____
_____
_____

Reflection Prompt: What are 3 ways I can take better care of my mental and emotional health?

_____
_____
_____

Week 12: Decision-Making & Problem-Solving

- Learn **effective decision-making strategies**.
- Practice **problem-solving techniques** through real-life scenarios.
- Create a **personal decision-making plan** for long-term success.

Decision-Making Plan Worksheet

Every day, you make decisions that move you forward—or pull you back. This worksheet helps you think through choices with intention, not impulse. Let's slow it down, break it down, and do it different this time.

Part 1: Think About Your Last Big Decision

What's the last decision you made that had real consequences—good or bad?

What was the outcome?

Would you make the same decision again? Why or why not?

Part 2: Your Go-To Decision Style

How do you usually make decisions? Check all that apply.

- ☐ I go with my gut
- ☐ I ask others first
- ☐ I act fast and deal with the results later
- ☐ I avoid deciding until I have to
- ☐ I write things down or talk it out
- ☐ I think it through before I act
- ☐ I look at how it affects my future
- ☐ I do what feels good in the moment

Part 3: Try the 4-Step Method

Use this simple method for your next big decision. Practice it below.

1. **What's the situation? (The choice you need to make)**

   _____

2. **What are my options? (List at least 2)**
   - Option 1: _____
   - Option 2: _____
   - Optional: Option 3: _____
3. **What are the possible outcomes of each option?**

   _____

4. **Which choice lines up with my goals and peace of mind?**

   _____

Decision Made: _____

_____

Part 4: When It Gets Hard...

If I feel pressured or overwhelmed, I will...
☐ Take a walk
☐ Write it down
☐ Call my support person
☐ Delay my decision
☐ Pray or reflect
☐ Use my workbook
☐ Other: _____

_____

Final Reflection

What decision are you facing right now—and how do you plan to handle it?

_____

What would change in your life if you made more intentional choices?

_____
_____

Weekly Reflection Journal – Week 12

Nobody's perfect. Mistakes don't mean failure—they mean you're learning. What did you figure out about yourself this week, even if it was messy?

This week, I made progress in:

_____
_____
_____

One challenge I faced was:

_____
_____
_____

Something I learned about myself was:

_____
_____
_____

My goal for next week is:

_____
_____
_____

Reflection Prompt: What's a decision I made in the past that taught me something?

_____
_____
_____

Phase 4: Financial Independence & Housing Stability (Weeks 13-16)

Goal: Strengthen financial management and housing security.

Week 13: Job Retention & Professional Growth

- Learn **workplace professionalism and career growth strategies.**
- Identify **opportunities for job advancement.**
- Develop a **long-term career plan.**

Career Plan Worksheet

Having a job pays the bills. Having a plan builds a future. Use this worksheet to figure out what type of work fits your life, your goals, and your strengths.

Part 1: What Have You Done?

List any past work experience (paid or unpaid):

Job / Task	Employer or Place	What You Did	Dates

What jobs or skills do you feel most confident doing?

_____

Part 2: What Are You Interested In?

Circle the fields or job types that interest you most:

- Warehouse / General Labor
- Customer Service
- Food Service / Restaurants
- Construction / Skilled Trades
- Cleaning / Maintenance
- Transportation (Uber, CDL, Delivery)
- Office / Clerical
- Healthcare
- Landscaping
- Youth or Community Work
- Entrepreneurship
- Other: _____

What kind of job fits your personality and values?

_____

Part 3: What's Holding You Back?

☐ I don't have a license
☐ I have a felony or criminal record
☐ I don't have a high school diploma or GED
☐ I don't know where to start
☐ I have health issues
☐ I need childcare
☐ I've never worked before
☐ I don't feel confident
☐ Other: _____

What support do you need to move forward?

_____
_____

Part 4: Training & Growth

Are there any trainings, certifications, or programs you want to look into?

☐ Forklift
☐ OSHA / Safety
☐ Food Handler's Card
☐ Peer Support Specialist
☐ CDL / Driving School
☐ Barber / Cosmetology
☐ CNA / Healthcare
☐ GED or College
☐ Other: _____

Part 5: Your 30-Day Job Plan

This month, I will: (check all that apply)
☐ Update or create a resume
☐ Apply to at least ___ jobs
☐ Follow up with places I applied
☐ Practice interview questions
☐ Ask for help with job search
☐ Visit a job fair or workforce center
☐ Stay consistent, even if I don't hear back

Final Reflection

What kind of future are you working toward—and how does a job fit into that vision?

_____
_____

Mental Health & Well-Being

Check in with yourself regularly. Circle how you feel today:

 Happy

 Neutral

 Stressed

 Sad

 Angry

 Tired

List three things you are grateful for today:

➢ _____
➢ _____
➢ _____

Weekly Reflection Journal – Week 13

It's one thing to get a job. It's another to keep it and grow in it. Think about what kind of worker—or leader—you want to be.

This week, I made progress in:

_____
_____
_____

One challenge I faced was:

_____
_____
_____

Something I learned about myself was:

_____
_____
_____

My goal for next week is:

_____
_____
_____

Reflection Prompt: What does it mean to "grow" in a job?

_____
_____
_____

Week 14: Credit Building & Financial Planning

- Learn **how to build and maintain good credit.**
- Create a **personal financial plan and savings goal.**
- Understand **debt management and responsible spending.**

Financial Plan Worksheet

Money isn't just about income—it's about control, peace of mind, and staying ready for life's ups and downs. Use this worksheet to create a real-life financial plan that supports your future.

Part 1: Where Are You Right Now?

Do you currently have any income?
☐ Yes   ☐ No
Source(s): _____

Do you have a bank account?
☐ Yes   ☐ No   ☐ I need help opening one

Do you owe money (debts, tickets, child support, loans)?
☐ Yes   ☐ No   If yes, describe:

_____

Part 2: Short-Term Financial Goals (Next 30–90 Days)

What are your financial priorities right now? Check all that apply:

☐ Catch up on rent or bills
☐ Open a savings account
☐ Get an ID or license
☐ Pay off fines / court costs
☐ Build credit
☐ Make a budget and stick to it
☐ Start saving for housing or transportation
☐ Other: _____

What's your #1 financial goal this month?

_____
_____

Part 3: Long-Term Financial Goals (Next 6–12 Months)

In the next year, I want to... (check all that apply)

☐ Have consistent income
☐ Build emergency savings
☐ Raise my credit score
☐ Eliminate major debt
☐ Buy a car or secure transportation
☐ Save for housing or deposit
☐ Get out of the check-to-check cycle
☐ Start a business or side hustle
☐ Other: _____

Part 4: My Monthly Financial Plan

Use this to build off your budget worksheet.

Expected Monthly Income: $_____
Total Monthly Expenses: $_____

Monthly Savings Goal: $_____
How much can you realistically save each week?
$_____

Where will you keep your savings?
☐ Bank   ☐ Prepaid Card   ☐ Cash Envelope   ☐ Other: _____

Part 5: Barriers & Solutions

What gets in the way of your financial goals?
☐ Overspending
☐ No stable income
☐ Emergency costs
☐ Lack of support or guidance
☐ I avoid thinking about money
☐ Other: _____

One thing I can do this week to move forward:
_____
_____

Final Reflection

What does financial stability look like to you?
_____
_____

Weekly Reflection Journal – Week 14

Credit, bills, loans—it can feel overwhelming. But you're not powerless. What's one thing you did this week to take back control?

This week, I made progress in:

_____
_____
_____

One challenge I faced was:

_____
_____
_____

Something I learned about myself was:

_____
_____
_____

My goal for next week is:

_____
_____
_____

Reflection Prompt: How can I start building my credit or managing debt?

_____
_____
_____

Week 15: Finalizing Housing Stability Plans

- Secure **long-term housing solutions**.
- Learn about **renter's rights and responsibilities**.
- Develop a **housing security plan**.

Housing Security Plan Worksheet

Having a place to live isn't just about shelter—it's about safety, peace, and stability. This worksheet helps you build a real plan to get housing, stay housed, or improve your living situation.

Part 1: Where Are You Now?

What is your current housing situation?
☐ Transitional housing
☐ Staying with friends/family
☐ Homeless / shelter
☐ Own or rent my own place
☐ Hotel or temporary arrangement
☐ Other: _____

How stable is it right now?
☐ Very stable   ☐ Somewhat stable   ☐ Not stable at all

Part 2: What Type of Housing Do You Want?

What kind of housing would meet your needs in the next 3–6 months?
☐ Shared housing / roommate
☐ 1-bedroom apartment
☐ Room for rent
☐ Sober living
☐ Housing through a program or voucher
☐ Return to family
☐ Other: _____

What's most important to you in a place to live?
☐ Affordability
☐ Safety
☐ Transportation access
☐ Near job or school
☐ Privacy
☐ Clean environment
☐ No drug activity
☐ Close to family or support

Part 3: What Are Your Barriers?

What could make it harder to find or keep housing? Check all that apply.

☐ Criminal record
☐ No income
☐ Poor credit history
☐ No ID or documentation
☐ Evictions or past-due rent
☐ Mental health or addiction challenges
☐ Lack of support
☐ Other: _____

Part 4: Housing Search Plan

What steps have you taken so far (or need to take)?

☐ Applied for housing programs
☐ Requested housing voucher / subsidy
☐ Collected documents (ID, SSN, pay stubs)
☐ Started searching online / calling landlords
☐ Talked to a case manager or housing navigator
☐ Created a budget for rent
☐ Contacted family/friends for temporary help

What will you do this week to move forward?

1. _____
2. _____
3. _____

Part 5: Staying Housed

Once you have housing, what will help you keep it?

☐ Budgeting and paying rent on time
☐ Setting boundaries with visitors
☐ Keeping the space clean
☐ Following house or lease rules
☐ Staying connected to case manager or support
☐ Avoiding conflict or risky behavior at home
☐ Reporting issues early (maintenance, safety)

2025 Pathway to Renewal (P2R) | www.Pathway2Renewal.org | All rights reserved.

What's one habit you can build now that will help you stay housed later?

_____
_____

Final Reflection

Why is stable housing important to your success in this program and in life?

_____
_____
_____

Weekly Reflection Journal – Week 15

Finding housing can feel like a full-time job. But if you're showing up and applying, you're building a foundation. Reflect on what you've done so far.

This week, I made progress in:

_____
_____
_____

One challenge I faced was:

_____
_____
_____

Something I learned about myself was:

_____
_____
_____

My goal for next week is:

_____
_____
_____

Reflection Prompt: What does housing stability look like for me long term?

_____
_____
_____

Week 16: Mental Wellness & Sustaining Independence

- Conduct a **final mental wellness check-in**.
- Develop a **personal independence and self-sufficiency plan**.

Personal Independence & Self-Sufficiency Plan

Being independent doesn't mean doing everything alone—it means being able to meet your needs, make decisions, and move forward without depending on systems or people who may not be reliable. This plan helps you figure out what independence looks like for you and how to build it.

Part 1: What Does Independence Mean to You?

In your own words, what does being independent mean?

_____
_____

What does "self-sufficiency" look like in your life? (Be real, not perfect.)

_____
_____

Part 2: Where Are You Right Now?

Check off what you are currently doing on your own or with minimal support:

☐ I have a safe place to live
☐ I manage my own money and bills
☐ I have my own form of transportation or way to get around
☐ I make my own appointments (doctor, court, case manager, etc.)
☐ I shop and cook for myself
☐ I can manage my medications or mental health needs
☐ I speak up for myself when I need something
☐ I'm working, in school, or actively job hunting
☐ I handle setbacks without falling apart
☐ I avoid situations and people that threaten my progress

What area do you feel strongest in right now?

_____

What area do you struggle with the most?

_____
_____

Part 3: What's Blocking You?

What are your current barriers to full independence? (Check all that apply)

- ☐ Unstable housing
- ☐ No job or inconsistent income
- ☐ Relying on family/friends too much
- ☐ Transportation problems
- ☐ Fear of being alone
- ☐ Poor time management
- ☐ Lack of confidence or motivation
- ☐ Health or mental health issues
- ☐ Legal restrictions or probation
- ☐ Other: _____

Part 4: Your Personal Independence Plan

What are 3 things you can focus on over the next 30 days to become more independent?

1. _____
2. _____
3. _____

What support or tools do you need to succeed?

Who can help hold you accountable?

Final Reflection

If you became fully self-sufficient, how would your life be different?

What would it feel like to truly depend on no one but yourself (and your support team by choice—not survival)?

Weekly Reflection Journal – Week 16

Independence isn't just about doing it alone—it's about knowing you can stand on your own. Where did you take charge this week?

This week, I made progress in:

_____
_____
_____

One challenge I faced was:

_____
_____
_____

Something I learned about myself was:

_____
_____
_____

My goal for next week is:

_____
_____

Reflection Prompt: What are signs I'm becoming more independent?

_____
_____
_____

2025 Pathway to Renewal (P2R) | www.Pathway2Renewal.org | All rights reserved.

Phase 5: Long-Term Success & Community Integration (Weeks 17-20)

Goal: Prepare participants for sustained independence and long-term success.

Week 17: Community Engagement & Social Support

- Learn how to **connect with community resources and support networks.**
- Explore **volunteer opportunities and mentorship programs.**
- Identify **ways to stay socially engaged** and avoid isolation.

Healing isn't something we're meant to do alone. People, programs, and purpose all play a role. This worksheet helps you think about who's in your corner—and how to build or rebuild connections that help you grow.

Part 1: Who's In Your Circle?

List people, programs, or spaces you feel connected to right now:

Name / Group / Program	Type of Support	Do You Feel Safe With Them?
		☐ Yes ☐ No ☐ Unsure
		☐ Yes ☐ No ☐ Unsure
		☐ Yes ☐ No ☐ Unsure

Is your current support system helping or hurting your growth? Why?

_____
_____

Part 2: Reconnecting Without Shame

Are there people you've lost contact with but want to reconnect to (friends, mentors, family)?
☐ Yes   ☐ No   ☐ Not sure

If yes, who?

_____

What held you back from reaching out?
☐ Pride
☐ Guilt or shame
☐ Burned bridges
☐ Fear of rejection
☐ Not ready
☐ Other: _____

What's one healthy relationship you'd like to repair or strengthen?
_____
_____

Part 3: Community & Belonging

What kind of community do you need to feel supported?
☐ Recovery or peer support
☐ Faith-based or spiritual groups
☐ Activism or social justice work
☐ Supportive work environment
☐ Education or trade school
☐ Creative or hobby-based groups
☐ Other: _____

What makes you feel like you *belong* somewhere?
_____
_____

Part 4: Next Steps

How will you build stronger connections this month? (Check 2 or more)
☐ Reach out to someone I trust
☐ Join a support group or program
☐ Volunteer or give back
☐ Spend time with people who lift me up
☐ Attend a community event
☐ Cut off people who drag me down
☐ Ask for help when I need it
☐ Other: _____

Final Reflection

What role does community play in your success and stability?
_____

Who or what do you want more of in your life moving forward?

Mental Health & Well-Being

Check in with yourself regularly. Circle how you feel today:

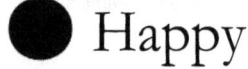 Happy

 Neutral

 Stressed

 Sad

 Angry

 Tired

List three things you are grateful for today:

➢ _____
➢ _____
➢ _____

Weekly Reflection Journal – Week 17

Support systems matter. Who showed up for you this week? Who didn't? What kind of support do you really need right now?

This week, I made progress in:

_____
_____
_____

One challenge I faced was:

_____
_____
_____

Something I learned about myself was:

_____
_____
_____

My goal for next week is:

_____
_____
_____

Reflection Prompt: Who are 3 people or places I can lean on for support after this program?

_____
_____
_____

Week 18: Advanced Financial Planning & Stability

- Learn **long-term financial strategies,** including **debt management and savings plans.**
- Understand **credit improvement techniques** and how to dispute inaccuracies.
- Develop a **three-year financial independence plan.**

3-Year Financial Independence Plan Worksheet

Financial independence isn't just about money—it's about freedom, stability, and choice. Use this worksheet to map out a 3-year vision, even if you're starting small. You don't have to have it all figured out—you just need a plan and the will to work it.

Part 1: What Does Financial Freedom Mean to You?

Describe what financial independence looks and feels like in your life:

- Where are you living?
- How are you making money?
- What's different about your stress, peace, and choices?

_____
_____
_____

Part 2: Your 3-Year Vision

In 3 years, I want to... *(check all that apply and fill in details)*

☐ Have steady income from work or business doing: _____
☐ Live in housing I can afford (rent or own)
☐ Have $_____ saved in the bank
☐ Be debt-free or managing debt responsibly
☐ Have strong credit and no collections
☐ Own a car / reliable transportation
☐ Support my family and kids without struggling
☐ Invest or build something for the future
☐ Other: _____

Part 3: What Could Get in the Way?

What barriers do you need to plan for or work through?
☐ Low income
☐ No savings
☐ Past-due debt or garnishments
☐ Legal issues
☐ Poor credit
☐ Inconsistent employment
☐ Spending habits
☐ Family or peer pressure
☐ Addiction / mental health challenges
☐ Other: _____

Part 4: Your 3-Year Roadmap

List 3 financial goals for each time frame below:

Next 6 Months

1. _____
2. _____
3. _____

Next 1 Year

1. _____
2. _____
3. _____

Next 3 Years

1. _____
2. _____
3. _____

Part 5: Habits to Start (or Stop) Now

List 2 habits you need to START and 2 habits you need to STOP to become financially independent.

Start:

1. _____
2. _____

Stop:

1. _____
2. _____

Final Reflection

How would your life feel different if money was no longer a daily stress?

_____

What would financial freedom allow you to do that you can't do now?

_____

Weekly Reflection Journal – Week 18

Emergencies don't wait until you're ready. Planning ahead takes pressure off your future self. What steps did you take this week to be more prepared?

This week, I made progress in:

_____
_____
_____

One challenge I faced was:

_____
_____
_____

Something I learned about myself was:

_____
_____
_____

My goal for next week is:

_____
_____
_____

Reflection Prompt: How can I plan for financial emergencies?

_____
_____
_____

Week 19: Personal Development & Self-Sufficiency

- Strengthen **problem-solving and decision-making skills**.
- Learn **self-advocacy techniques** for employment and housing stability.
- Develop **a personal wellness plan** for long-term mental health and emotional stability.

Personal Wellness Plan Worksheet

Wellness isn't just about feeling "okay"—it's about creating balance in your life so you can keep going, stay grounded, and move forward. This worksheet helps you build a plan to care for your mind, body, and spirit in ways that fit your real life.

Part 1: What Does Wellness Mean to You?

In your own words, what does being "well" or "healthy" look like for you—physically, mentally, emotionally, or spiritually?

_____
_____

What makes you feel off-balance or unhealthy most often?
☐ Stress ☐ Lack of sleep ☐ Poor eating habits
☐ Toxic people ☐ Feeling isolated ☐ Depression/anxiety
☐ Other: _____

Part 2: Rate Your Wellness Areas

On a scale of 1–5 (1 = needs major work, 5 = strong), how would you rate each area of your wellness today?

Wellness Area	Rating (1–5)
Physical Health	
Mental Health	
Spiritual Health / Faith	
Relationships	
Environment (home/living space)	
Work / Purpose	
Rest / Relaxation	

Weekly Reflection Journal – Week 19

Using your voice isn't always easy, especially if it's been ignored in the past. How did you stand up for yourself this week?

This week, I made progress in:

_____
_____
_____

One challenge I faced was:

_____
_____
_____

Something I learned about myself was:

_____
_____
_____

My goal for next week is:

_____
_____
_____

Reflection Prompt: How can I speak up for myself without conflict?

_____
_____
_____

Week 20: Long-Term Stability & Success Planning

- Reflect on your progress so far and recommit to your goals.
- Identify what's working and what needs to be reinforced.
- Start mapping out the life you want to build beyond the program.
- Begin preparing key pieces (housing, income, support) for life after Week 26.

Long-Term Stability & Success Plan

You're past the halfway mark, and you're still here. That means something. This worksheet helps you start thinking ahead—not about graduating, but about what comes next and how to build a life that lasts. Let's get intentional about your next 6 months and beyond.

Part 1: What's Working So Far?

What are 3 things that have helped you stay committed to this program?

1. _____
2. _____
3. _____

What habits or changes do you want to protect long-term?
☐ Waking up early ☐ Journaling ☐ Managing my money
☐ Staying sober ☐ Avoiding certain people ☐ Keeping structure
☐ Asking for help ☐ Setting boundaries ☐ Other: _____

Part 2: 6-Month Stability Plan

What do you want your life to look like 6 months from now?
(Housing, income, relationships, mindset, etc.)

_____
_____

Part 3: Start Thinking Ahead

Which of these do you need to prepare for before this program ends? (Check all that apply)
☐ Securing housing
☐ Steady income or job placement
☐ Staying clean or in recovery
☐ Transitioning to outpatient support or therapy
☐ Avoiding unhealthy environments
☐ Rebuilding family relationships
☐ Having ID, benefits, and legal docs ready
☐ Mental health or medication support
☐ Saving money or budgeting
☐ Planning for child care
☐ Getting a driver's license or car

☐ Building a healthy routine
☐ Other: _____

Part 4: The "Now vs. Later" List

What do you still need to work on now (during the program)?

1. _____
2. _____
3. _____

What are things you need to plan for later (after graduation)?

1. _____
2. _____
3. _____

Reflection Prompt

What scares you most about life after this program—and what will you do to stay focused and strong anyway?

_____
_____

Note to Participant:

We're not done. But we are preparing. The next 6 weeks will help you strengthen your independence, build legacy, and get ready to thrive beyond these walls. You got this.

Weekly Reflection Journal – Week 20

This journey hasn't been easy—but you're still standing. Look back and reflect on something you never thought you'd get through—but you did.

This week, I made progress in:

_____
_____
_____

One challenge I faced was:

_____
_____
_____

Something I learned about myself was:

_____
_____
_____

My goal for next week is:

_____
_____
_____

Reflection Prompt: What's something I've done this year that I never thought I could do?

_____
_____
_____

Phase 6: Wellness, Legacy, and Lifelong Success (Weeks 21–26)

Goal: Prepare participants for life beyond the program by focusing on wellness, identity, self-advocacy, legal stability, and long-term independence. This phase helps participants solidify their growth, celebrate their progress, and map out a sustainable future.

Week 21: Physical Health & Wellness Foundations

Goal: Build awareness around physical wellness and how it connects to long-term independence and mental clarity.

Daily Tasks:

- Schedule or attend a health or dental check-up.
- Track your medications, appointments, and physical health needs.
- Learn about meal planning, sleep hygiene, and basic physical activity.

Participant Assignments:

- Complete the *Personal Health & Wellness Checklist*.
- Identify one health goal and one health-related barrier.
- Locate a free or low-cost health resource in your community.

Worksheet: Personal Health & Wellness Tracker

Personal Health & Wellness Checklist

You don't have to be perfect to take care of yourself—but ignoring your health can hold you back. This checklist will help you take a full-body, full-life inventory and make a plan for feeling better, stronger, and more in control.

Part 1: Physical Health Check-In

Do you currently have a doctor or primary care provider?
☐ Yes   ☐ No   ☐ Not sure

When was your last…

- Physical exam: _____
- Dental visit: _____
- Vision check: _____
- Blood pressure check: _____
- STI/HIV test: _____
- COVID/flu shots: _____

Check any of these you've experienced recently:
☐ Frequent pain or fatigue
☐ Trouble sleeping
☐ Changes in weight or appetite
☐ Missed medications
☐ Shortness of breath or chest pain
☐ No insurance or access to care
☐ No transportation to get to the doctor

Do you need help getting medical care?
☐ Yes   ☐ No   If yes, what kind? _____

Part 2: Mental & Emotional Wellness

How are you managing your mental health right now?
☐ I'm in therapy or peer support
☐ I use healthy coping skills
☐ I have someone I can talk to
☐ I keep things bottled up
☐ I feel overwhelmed or anxious often
☐ I've had thoughts of harming myself or others
☐ I'm working on it, but I need more support

What coping tools work best for you?
☐ Journaling ☐ Talking it out
☐ Walking or exercise ☐ Spiritual practices
☐ Listening to music ☐ Support groups
☐ Other: _____

Part 3: Substance Use & Recovery (if applicable)

Have you used any substances (drugs, alcohol) in the past 30 days?
☐ Yes ☐ No ☐ In recovery

Are you currently in a recovery program or support group?
☐ Yes ☐ No ☐ Looking for one

Do you have a relapse prevention or support plan?
☐ Yes ☐ No ☐ I need help making one

Part 4: Healthy Habits Tracker

Which of these healthy habits are part of your weekly routine?
☐ Drinking water daily
☐ Eating balanced meals
☐ Moving or exercising a few times a week
☐ Getting 6–8 hours of sleep
☐ Taking medications as prescribed
☐ Limiting screen time
☐ Saying "no" to toxic people
☐ Attending support groups or appointments
☐ Taking time to rest or recharge

Part 5: What Needs Attention?

List 2 areas of your health or wellness you need to improve:

1. _____
2. _____

What's one small step you can take this week to get started?

_____
_____

Final Reflection

If your body and mind felt better, what would change in your daily life?

_____

_____

Personal Health & Wellness Tracker

Wellness isn't about perfection—it's about paying attention to what you need, one day at a time. Use this tracker to check in with your body, mind, and habits for one full week. Circle or fill in what applies each day. Be honest. This is for you.

Part 1: Daily Check-In (Weekly Grid)

Day	Slept 6–8 Hrs	Ate 2+ Meals	Took Meds (if any)	Drank Water	Moved My Body	Felt Calm / Balanced	Reached Out to Someone	Avoided Substances	Kept My Boundaries
Monday	☐	☐	☐	☐	☐	☐	☐	☐	☐
Tuesday	☐	☐	☐	☐	☐	☐	☐	☐	☐
Wednesday	☐	☐	☐	☐	☐	☐	☐	☐	☐
Thursday	☐	☐	☐	☐	☐	☐	☐	☐	☐
Friday	☐	☐	☐	☐	☐	☐	☐	☐	☐
Saturday	☐	☐	☐	☐	☐	☐	☐	☐	☐
Sunday	☐	☐	☐	☐	☐	☐	☐	☐	☐

Part 2: Weekly Reflection

What wellness habit did you stick to the most this week? Why?

_____

Where did you struggle most? What got in the way?

_____

How did you feel by the end of the week—physically and mentally?

_____
_____

Part 3: Plan for Next Week

One thing I'll continue doing next week:

_____

One thing I want to improve:

_____

Someone I can talk to or ask for support:

_____
_____

Reminder:

Progress doesn't always feel big—but showing up for yourself in small ways, every day, is how you win long-term.

_____

Mental Health & Well-Being

Check in with yourself regularly. Circle how you feel today:

 Happy

 Neutral

 Stressed

 Sad

 Angry

 Tired

List three things you are grateful for today:

➢ _____
➢ _____
➢ _____

Weekly Reflection Journal – Week 21

Taking care of your body helps your mind too. Even small things matter. What did you do this week to treat your body with care?

This week, I made progress in:

_____
_____
_____

One challenge I faced was:

_____
_____
_____

Something I learned about myself was:

_____
_____
_____

My goal for next week is:

_____
_____
_____

Reflection Prompt: How does taking care of my physical health help me grow?

_____
_____
_____

Week 22: Legal Preparedness & Documentation Recovery

Goal: Remove legal barriers to progress and ensure documentation needed for work, housing, and independence is in place.

Daily Tasks:

- Review your legal history and current needs with staff.
- Apply for or recover missing documents (ID, SS card, birth certificate).
- Learn the basics of legal rights and record expungement.

Participant Assignments:

- Complete the *Legal Preparedness Checklist*.
- Make a plan to get missing documents and schedule any legal appointments.
- Connect with a legal aid or community law clinic, if applicable.

Worksheet: Legal Preparedness & Documentation Plan

Legal Preparedness & Documentation Plan

Being prepared legally means having your paperwork in order, knowing your rights, and having a plan if something comes up. This worksheet helps you track what you have, what you need, and how to protect yourself moving forward.

Part 1: Vital Documents Checklist

Check what you currently have and what you still need:

Document	Have It? ☐	Need It? ☐	Notes / Expiration Date
Photo ID / State ID			
Social Security Card			
Birth Certificate			
Health Insurance Card			
Medicaid/Medicare Card			
Voter Registration Card			
SNAP/EBT Card			
Child Custody or Support Papers			
Housing Voucher / Lease Agreement			
Probation or Parole Paperwork			
Court Orders / Discharge Documents			
Resume / Job Records / Certifications			
Other:			

Do you need help getting any documents above?
☐ Yes   ☐ No   If yes, explain:

_____
_____

Part 2: Legal Status & Goals

Are you currently on probation or parole?
☐ Yes   ☐ No   If yes, until when? _____

Are you facing any open cases or charges?
☐ Yes   ☐ No   ☐ Not sure

Do you have unpaid fines, tickets, or fees?
☐ Yes   ☐ No   If yes, amount: $_____

Do you have a plan to resolve legal issues?
☐ Yes   ☐ No   If yes, what's your next step?

_____
_____

Part 3: Action Steps to Get Legally Ready

What legal or document-related tasks do you need to complete in the next 30 days?

1. _____
2. _____
3. _____

Who can help you complete these tasks?
☐ Case manager
☐ Program staff
☐ Public defender
☐ Legal aid / reentry service
☐ Family member or friend
☐ Other: _____

_____

Final Reflection

Why is legal preparedness important for your future stability?

_____

How will having your documents in order help you with housing, work, or benefits?

_____

Weekly Reflection Journal – Week 22

It's hard to focus on the future when the past keeps knocking. What's one legal or paperwork step you took to move forward?

This week, I made progress in:

_____
_____
_____

One challenge I faced was:

_____
_____
_____

Something I learned about myself was:

_____
_____
_____

My goal for next week is:

_____
_____
_____

Reflection Prompt: What can I do now to protect my future legally?

_____
_____
_____

Week 23: Giving Back & Building Legacy

Goal: Explore personal purpose, legacy, and the power of giving back to others and the community.

Daily Tasks:

- Participate in a volunteer activity or help someone in need.
- Reflect on the kind of example or legacy you want to leave behind.
- Identify ways you can be a role model or positive influence.

Participant Assignments:

- Complete the *Legacy Mapping Worksheet*.
- Volunteer at least one hour this week.
- Identify one younger person or peer you can support or mentor.

Worksheet: Legacy & Community Impact Plan

Legacy & Community Impact Plan

You've come through struggle—and you're still standing. That alone is powerful. But legacy isn't just what you leave behind when you're gone—it's what you build every day. This worksheet helps you think about how to turn your pain, progress, and experience into purpose.

Part 1: Define Your Legacy

When people speak about you in the future, what do you want them to say?

_____
_____

What values or lessons do you want to pass on?
☐ Resilience ☐ Accountability ☐ Faith
☐ Discipline ☐ Giving Back ☐ Growth
☐ Breaking Generational Cycles
☐ Other: _____

Part 2: Who Are You Impacting Right Now?

Who's watching you—whether you realize it or not?
☐ Children / family members
☐ Younger siblings
☐ Friends from back home
☐ Others in recovery or transition
☐ People in your community
☐ Nobody right now—but I want to change that

What have they already seen you overcome?

_____
_____

2025 Pathway to Renewal (P2R) | www.Pathway2Renewal.org | All rights reserved.

Part 3: Giving Back

How do you want to make a difference in your community? (Choose all that apply)

- ☐ Mentor someone younger than me
- ☐ Volunteer or give time to a cause
- ☐ Start a small business or hustle to support my neighborhood
- ☐ Speak to youth or at-risk individuals
- ☐ Use my story to inspire or teach
- ☐ Help others transition from prison, addiction, or homelessness
- ☐ Other: _____

What's something small you can do in the next 30 days to give back?

_____
_____

Part 4: Your Legacy Statement

Write a short paragraph that sums up the legacy you're working toward. This can be about your family, community, faith, or personal values. Make it real. Make it yours.

"I want to be remembered as someone who…"

_____
_____
_____
_____

Final Reflection

Why does it matter to leave something behind bigger than yourself?

_____

How will living with purpose help you stay focused after this program?

_____

Weekly Reflection Journal – Week 23

Giving back doesn't have to be big. It can be a kind word, a helping hand. What's something you did this week that helped someone else?

This week, I made progress in:

_____
_____
_____

One challenge I faced was:

_____
_____
_____

Something I learned about myself was:

_____
_____
_____

My goal for next week is:

_____
_____
_____

Reflection Prompt: What does "giving back" mean to me, and how will I do it?

_____
_____
_____

Week 24: Personal Branding & Storytelling

Goal: Help participants take ownership of their narrative and prepare to present themselves professionally and powerfully.

Daily Tasks:

- Practice telling your story from a position of strength.
- Develop a short elevator pitch for interviews or networking.
- Learn how to write or share your story for empowerment.

Participant Assignments:

- Write a personal redemption or success story.
- Create a 60-second elevator pitch.
- Identify opportunities to share your story (support groups, interviews, etc.).

Worksheet: Telling My Story – Personal Narrative Tool

Storytelling & Personal Narrative Tool

Your story isn't just what happened to you—it's what you did with it. This tool helps you organize your life experiences into a personal story that's honest, healing, and powerful. You don't have to be perfect—just real.

Part 1: Break Your Story Into 3 Parts

1. Where You Were
Think about your background, environment, or the struggle you were facing.

"Before this program, my life looked like…"

_____
_____

2. What Changed You
Name the turning point—an event, a decision, a consequence, or a moment of realization.

"Things started to change when…"

_____
_____

3. Where You're Headed Now
Talk about the growth, progress, and goals you have now.

"Today, I'm focused on…"

_____
_____
_____

Part 2: Own Your Strengths

What are 3 things you've survived or overcome?

1. _____
2. _____
3. _____

What did those experiences teach you about yourself?

_____
_____

Part 3: Identify Your Message

If someone was hearing your story for the first time, what do you want them to feel or learn?
☐ Hope
☐ Courage
☐ Accountability
☐ Healing
☐ Second chances
☐ Power to change
☐ Other: _____

My story teaches people that…

_____
_____

Part 4: Practice Your Voice

Fill in the blanks below to build a short version of your personal story (2–3 minutes max):

"My name is _____, and I come from _____.
I've been through _____, but I didn't give up.
What helped me grow was _____.
Today, I'm focused on _____ and I'm proud of how far I've come.
If you take anything from my story, let it be this: _____."

_____

Final Reflection

How does it feel to take control of your story instead of letting your past control you?

_____

Where or when would you like to share your story in the future?
☐ Job interview   ☐ Group session   ☐ Youth program
☐ Recovery space   ☐ Court / legal advocacy   ☐ Social media
☐ Other: _____

Weekly Reflection Journal – Week 24

Your story matters—even the messy parts. Think about how far you've come. If you had to tell someone your journey, what would you say?

This week, I made progress in:

_____
_____
_____

One challenge I faced was:

_____
_____
_____

Something I learned about myself was:

_____
_____
_____

My goal for next week is:

_____
_____
_____

Reflection Prompt: What part of my story shows how far I've come?

_____
_____
_____

Week 25: Exit Planning & Alumni Readiness

Goal: Organize resources, create a post-program routine, and finalize the transition plan for ongoing success.

Daily Tasks:

- Finalize housing, job, and therapy support referrals.
- Identify emergency contacts and backup resources.
- Meet with your program provider to review progress.

Participant Assignments:

- Complete the *30-Day Post-Program Plan*.
- Identify 3 go-to people or organizations you will check in with.
- Review workbook and progress with your provider.

Worksheet: Alumni Transition & Support Plan

Alumni Transition & Support Plan

You've almost made it through the program—but the real work starts when the structure fades. This plan helps you build a support system, create routine, and stay connected so you don't lose everything you've worked for. You didn't come this far just to go back.

Part 1: What Are You Walking Away With?

What are the top 3 things you've gained from this program?

1. _____
2. _____
3. _____

What habits or routines do you want to continue after graduation?
☐ Journaling ☐ Budgeting
☐ Asking for help ☐ Support groups
☐ Staying sober ☐ Following a daily routine
☐ Boundaries ☐ Therapy or peer support
☐ Other: _____

Part 2: Post-Program Routine

What will your typical weekday look like after graduation?

Time of Day	Activity or Focus
Morning (7–10 AM)	
Midday (10 AM–2 PM)	
Afternoon (2–6 PM)	
Evening (6–10 PM)	

What will keep you on schedule?
☐ Calendar / planner ☐ Alarm reminders
☐ Accountability partner ☐ Structured job or program
☐ Other: _____

Part 3: Staying Connected After Graduation

How will you stay connected to the support system you've built? (Check all that apply)
☐ Join the P2R Alumni Network
☐ Keep in touch with peer support staff
☐ Continue therapy or outpatient care
☐ Meet with mentor or sponsor regularly
☐ Attend weekly check-in calls or groups
☐ Volunteer or give back to the program
☐ Other: _____

Who are 2 people you can reach out to when you feel off track?

1. _____
2. _____

Part 4: Watch Out for the Red Flags

What signs will let you know you're slipping? (Check your personal red flags)
☐ Skipping appointments
☐ Isolating or ghosting people
☐ Returning to risky environments
☐ Lying or hiding what you're going through
☐ Not eating or sleeping right
☐ Mood swings or outbursts
☐ Drug/alcohol urges
☐ Other: _____

What will you do if these signs show up?
☐ Call someone I trust   ☐ Revisit my workbook
☐ Ask for help   ☐ Go back to group
☐ Pause and reflect   ☐ Other: _____

Part 5: My Transition Statement

"After this program, I plan to _____
with the help of _____.
I know life will still have challenges, but I'm choosing to _____
because I believe _____."

Final Reflection

What do you want to be true about your life 6 months from now—and how will you make sure you don't lose your progress?

_____
_____

Weekly Reflection Journal – Week 25

Graduation is close. What support system will you need to keep moving forward? Who's in your corner when this program ends?

This week, I made progress in:

_____
_____
_____

One challenge I faced was:

_____
_____
_____

Something I learned about myself was:

_____
_____
_____

My goal for next week is:

_____
_____
_____

Reflection Prompt: What support system will help me stay focused after graduation?

_____
_____
_____

2025 Pathway to Renewal (P2R) | www.Pathway2Renewal.org | All rights reserved.

Week 26: Graduation & Giving Yourself Credit

Focus: Celebrate progress, lock in confidence, and commit to continued growth.

Daily Tasks:

- Participate in your graduation session or celebration.
- Write a letter to yourself (or someone who supported you) about how far you've come.
- Practice a gratitude ritual or reflection exercise.

Participant Assignments:

- Complete the *Final Program Reflection*.
- Write a thank-you note to someone who helped you along the way.
- Consider becoming a peer mentor or alumni support member.

Worksheet: Final Reflection Letter & Gratitude Statement

Self-Check: Where Am I Now? (Week 26 – Post-Program Comparison)

This is your moment to pause and check in—honestly. You've been doing the work. This page is for *you* to see how far you've come since Week 1. There's no right or wrong—just truth.

Part 1: Rate Where You Are Today

Circle how you feel in each area right now.
(1 = struggling, 5 = strong & steady)

Life Area	1	2	3	4	5
Mental Health	☐	☐	☐	☐	☐
Emotional Control	☐	☐	☐	☐	☐
Physical Health	☐	☐	☐	☐	☐
Sobriety / Substance Use	☐	☐	☐	☐	☐
Housing Stability	☐	☐	☐	☐	☐
Employment / Income	☐	☐	☐	☐	☐
Motivation / Focus	☐	☐	☐	☐	☐
Time Management & Structure	☐	☐	☐	☐	☐
Relationships & Support Network	☐	☐	☐	☐	☐
Confidence in My Future	☐	☐	☐	☐	☐

Part 2: Open Reflection

What's one area where you've grown the most?

What area still needs work—but you're more aware of it now?

_____

What are you proud of yourself for doing differently?

_____
_____

Part 3: Personal Milestones

In this program, I have... (Check all that apply)
- ☐ Gotten stable housing
- ☐ Started working or school
- ☐ Built a healthy routine
- ☐ Stayed sober or clean
- ☐ Improved my mental health
- ☐ Reconnected with family
- ☐ Set personal boundaries
- ☐ Created a budget or savings plan
- ☐ Avoided jail or hospital stays
- ☐ Found purpose or faith
- ☐ Learned to ask for help
- ☐ Other: _____

Final Thought

Finish this sentence:

"Now that I've completed this program, I believe I am..."

_____
_____
_____

Final Reflection Letter & Gratitude Statement

Week 26 – Completion & Closing

Final Reflection Letter

You've made it. You showed up for yourself—even when it was hard. This is your time to reflect, give thanks, and close this chapter with strength, purpose, and pride.

Write a letter to yourself, your support system, or anyone who needs to hear your truth. This is your story. This is your power.

You can include:

- What this program meant to you
- How you've changed since Week 1
- What you're proud of
- What you're still working on
- Your hopes for the future

Start your letter below:

"When I first started this program, I was…"

"The hardest part of this journey was…"

"The moment I knew I was growing was…"

"Now, I'm leaving this program with…"

"To anyone who's struggling like I was, I would say…"

"I'm not perfect, but I am _____."

"And I'm proud of myself because…"

"Here's what's next for me…"

(Feel free to continue this letter in your journal or write on the back of this page.)

Gratitude Statement

List 3 things you're truly grateful for as you complete this program:

1. _____
2. _____
3. _____

Who do you want to thank?
(Check all that apply or write in names below)

☐ Myself (for not giving up)
☐ My peer support or therapist
☐ My family or loved ones
☐ The program staff
☐ My higher power / faith
☐ A fellow participant
☐ Other: _____

Final Thought

You are **not who you were** when you started.
You're **better. Wiser. Still becoming.**

Congratulations.
You're not just finishing something—you're stepping into something greater.
This is your time.
Keep going. We believe in you.

Thank-You Note

Sometimes just saying "thank you" is powerful. Use this space to write a short note to someone who helped you along the way. You can give it to them—or just keep it as a reminder of who showed up for you.

_____

Who are you writing to?
(Name or role: e.g., "My peer support specialist," "Ms. Kendra," "My sister"):

_____
_____

Write your note below:

Dear _____,

I just want to say thank you.

When I was going through _____,

you were there to _____.

You may not even realize how much that meant to me.

Because of your support, I've been able to _____.

I'm not done yet, but I'm moving forward—and I'm grateful.

Thank you for believing in me when I didn't always believe in myself.

With respect and gratitude,

_____

(Your name)

Step Into Leadership: Give Back as a Peer Mentor or Alumni Support

You've been through the storm—and now you're walking out stronger. That's powerful. And someone else out there is just starting their journey, feeling lost like you once did.

You can be the reason they keep going.

As a **Peer Mentor** or **Alumni Support Member**, you can:

- Share your story to inspire others
- Help new participants adjust to the program
- Offer real advice from real experience
- Stay connected to a community that still needs you

You don't have to be perfect to lead—you just have to be honest, committed, and willing to show up.

If you're interested in giving back, talk to your program director or peer support coordinator about how to get involved after graduation.

You've made it this far. Now imagine who you could help walk this same path.

Weekly Reflection Journal – Week 26

You did this. Not perfectly, maybe not fast—but you finished. Look at where you started and where you are now. What are you most proud of?

This week, I made progress in:

_____
_____
_____

One challenge I faced was:

_____
_____
_____

Something I learned about myself was:

_____
_____
_____

My goal for next week is:

_____
_____
_____

Reflection Prompt: What am I most proud of in my journey?

_____
_____
_____

Stay Connected: Join the Pathway to Renewal Alumni Network

Your journey doesn't end here—and it shouldn't be walked alone.
Graduates of the Pathway to Renewal (P2R) program are invited to stay connected, support others, and continue growing by joining the **P2R Alumni Network and Peer Support Community**.

Why Build a Community?

Graduating is a major milestone—but lasting success comes from **staying rooted in support, structure, and purpose**. By creating a peer-led alumni network, we're building something bigger than a program:
We're building a movement.

Benefits of Joining or Starting a P2R Support Group:

- **Stay connected** to like-minded individuals who understand your journey
- **Receive and give encouragement** during life's transitions
- **Access resources** for housing, jobs, wellness, and reentry support
- **Participate in workshops, alumni meetups, and check-in circles**
- **Mentor new participants** who are just starting the path you've already walked
- **Amplify your voice** and shape the future of the P2R movement

---

How to Get Involved:

- Talk to your program coordinator or peer support team about starting or joining an alumni circle
- Volunteer as a **group facilitator**, **mentor**, or **resource sharer**
- Attend quarterly alumni calls or in-person meetups
- Be part of something that doesn't end with graduation—it grows with you

---

Together, we're not just changing lives—we're building a new standard of healing, support, and success. One person at a time. One community at a time.

Appendix

Job Application Tracker

Use this table to track your job applications and interviews.

Date	Company Name	Position Applied For	Contact Info	Status/Follow-Up	Notes

2025 Pathway to Renewal (P2R) | www.Pathway2Renewal.org | All rights reserved.

Housing Search Log

Date Contacted	Property/Location	Rent Amount	Contact Info	Application Submitted?	Outcome	Notes

Daily Routine Planning

Creating structure in your day is important. Fill out this schedule to plan your daily activities.

Time	Activity
6:00 AM	_____
9:00 AM	_____
12:00 PM	_____
3:00 PM	_____
6:00 PM	_____
9:00 PM	_____

Crisis & Safety Plan

This section is your personal Crisis & Safety Plan. It's designed to help you—and those who support you—know what to do if you start feeling overwhelmed or in crisis. Fill this out with your therapist, peer support specialist, or on your own, and keep it updated.

Client Name: _____
Date of Birth: _____
Date Completed: _____
Staff/Clinician Name: _____
Service Type: ☐ CST ☐ Peer Support ☐ Outpatient Therapy ☐ Other: _____

1. Triggers or Warning Signs

What events or feelings suggest that a crisis may be developing?

- _____
- _____
- _____

2. Crisis Responses

Thoughts, feelings, or behaviors I may experience in a crisis:

- _____
- _____
- _____

3. Coping Strategies I Can Use Independently

- _____
- _____
- _____

4. Support Contacts

People I can call for help and support:

Name	Relationship	Phone Number

5. Community Resources

Agencies or hotlines I can contact in a crisis:

Resource	Service	Phone
Mobile Crisis	On-site response	
988 Crisis Line	24/7 crisis support	988
TSG Behavioral Health	Peer, therapy, case mgmt.	(704) 553-5392
Other:		

6. What Helps Me Feel Safe

- _____
- _____
- _____

7. What Makes Things Worse

- _____
- _____
- _____

8. Preferred Crisis Interventions

Things others should know when assisting me in crisis:

- _____
- _____
- _____

9. After-Crisis Recovery Plan

How I will move forward after a crisis:

- _____
- _____

Grievance & Complaint Process

What if I have a concern about my services or how I've been treated?

You have the right to file a grievance or complaint at any time without fear of punishment or losing services. This can include concerns about how you were treated by staff, delays in services, or your rights not being respected.

Step 1: Tell Your Provider

Start by speaking with someone at the agency providing your services. Ask for a supervisor or manager to help you. Every agency is required to have a formal grievance process.

You may submit your complaint verbally or in writing. Ask for a copy of your provider's grievance policy if you haven't received one.

Step 2: Contact Your Local LME/MCO

If you are not satisfied with how your provider handled the complaint—or don't feel comfortable speaking with them—you may contact your **Local Management Entity/Managed Care Organization (LME/MCO).**

Your LME/MCO: _____

(Staff can write this in during onboarding)

You may also call the

NC DHHS Customer Service and Advocacy Office:

📞 **Toll-Free:** 1-800-662-7030 ● **Hours:** 8:00 AM – 5:00 PM, Monday – Friday

Website: www.ncdhhs.gov

Note: If your concern is about abuse, neglect, exploitation, or safety, you can also contact:

- **Local DSS (Department of Social Services)**
- **NC Division of Health Service Regulation Complaint Intake:** 1-800-624-3004

Your voice matters. You will not lose services or be treated unfairly for using your rights.

Helpful Numbers & Personal Contacts

Use this page to keep track of important phone numbers and support contacts. Bring it to appointments or keep it somewhere easy to find.

Contact Type	Name	Phone Number	Notes
Therapist / Counselor			
Peer Support Specialist			
Case Manager			
Psychiatrist			
Crisis Line (Mobile Crisis)			Available 24/7
988 Suicide & Crisis Lifeline		**988**	
Pharmacy			
Primary Doctor			
Family/Friend for Support			
LME/MCO Customer Service			
			Available 24/7

Pathway to Renewal (P2R) – Logic Model

This logic model explains how the P2R program creates long-term change by guiding individuals through structured, trauma-informed services that promote stability, healing, and community reintegration. This page shows how the entire P2R program works to create change—from support to results.

---

1. Inputs (Resources)

- Trained peer support specialists, therapists, and case managers
- Participant workbook and 26-week structured curriculum
- Transitional housing and case management support
- Community partnerships (job training, legal aid, recovery resources)
- Medicaid billing and nonprofit grants

---

2. Activities

- Weekly one-on-one and group check-ins
- Phase-based personal development (Stabilization → Legacy)
- Life skills development (e.g., budgeting, housing search, legal prep)
- Mental health support, journaling, and trauma-informed care
- Job search coaching and benefits navigation
- Alumni mentorship and goal planning

---

3. Outputs

- Completion of 26-week personal development program
- Participant workbooks filled with weekly reflections and tools
- Progress in housing, income, mental wellness, and legal readiness
- Ongoing data collection using pre/post assessments

---

4. Short-Term Outcomes (0–6 Months)

- Improved emotional regulation and coping skills
- Stabilized housing and consistent income
- Increased personal insight and future planning
- Re-engagement with support systems and community

---

5. Long-Term Outcomes (6+ Months)

- Reduced recidivism and reliance on crisis systems
- Sustained employment or educational growth
- Stronger relationships and personal accountability
- Empowered alumni serving as mentors or peer support
- Increased long-term mental health stability and life satisfaction

Research-Based Program Foundations
Evidence-Based Foundations of P2R

Why P2R Works

The **Pathway to Renewal (P2R)** program is grounded in evidence-based practices used by leading behavioral health and reentry organizations across the U.S. It combines therapeutic models, public health frameworks, and recovery-oriented strategies to support long-term change. This guide draws directly from principles recognized by:
- **SAMHSA** – Substance Abuse and Mental Health Services Administration
- **NC DHHS** – North Carolina Department of Health and Human Services
- **HUD** – U.S. Department of Housing and Urban Development

Core Models That Shape P2R

- **Trauma-Informed Care** – ensures emotional safety and client choice
- **SAMHSA's Eight Dimensions of Wellness** – supports whole-person health
- **Motivational Interviewing (MI)** – supports behavior change with empathy
- **Strength-Based & Person-Centered Planning** – focuses on goals and capacity, not deficits
- **Housing First Principles (HUD)** – stability is the foundation for recovery
- **Cognitive Behavioral Techniques (CBT)** – challenge thinking, shift behavior

These frameworks are applied in a way that is **accessible, real-world**, and **non-clinical**—helping participants develop structure, insight, and tools they can actually use.

P2R also reflects research-backed priorities outlined in:
- **SAMHSA's Recovery Support Strategic Initiative**
- **HUD's National Strategy to Prevent and End Homelessness**
- **NC DHHS Justice-Involved Behavioral Health models**

P2R isn't just "inspired" by these frameworks — it actively reflects them.

Evidence-Based Model	Corresponding P2R Tools/Features
Trauma-Informed Care	Crisis Plan, Emotional Check-Ins, Soft Language
Eight Dimensions of Wellness	Worksheets for all 8 domains
Motivational Interviewing	Weekly prompts, self-driven reflections, autonomy
Cognitive Behavioral Techniques	Conflict tools, routine tracking, reframing exercises
Person-Centered Planning	Participant-led goals, flexible engagement
HUD's Housing First	Housing focus from Week 1, non-conditional support approach

About the Author

Dr. Kerry L. Shipman, J.D., Ph.D., MPA, CADC, PMP
Executive Director, TSG Behavioral Health & Community Services
Founder, The Black Therapy Network | Program Creator, Pathway to Renewal

Dr. Kerry L. Shipman is a highly credentialed behavioral health executive, professor, and justice reform advocate with over 15 years of cross-sector leadership in the fields of criminal justice, mental health, and community reentry.

He is the Executive Director of TSG Behavioral Health & Community Services, a Medicaid-enrolled provider agency focused on transitional support for justice-involved and underserved individuals. Dr. Shipman also founded The Black Therapy Network, a culturally responsive mental health platform that increases access to therapy for African Americans by offering affordable, stigma-free care led by Black clinicians.

A former North Carolina magistrate judge and former project lead at the NC Department of Health and Human Services (NC DHHS), Dr. Shipman's work spans government, education, and nonprofit systems. He holds a Ph.D. in Criminal Justice, a Juris Doctorate, a Master of Public Administration, and nationally recognized credentials in Addiction Counseling (CADC) and Project Management (PMP).

He is also a professor of criminal justice and political science, known for fusing academic rigor with lived experience. Featured in Yahoo Finance, Black Enterprise, WFMZ, and The Bencher, his work centers on reentry, equity, and the practical transformation of systems that often overlook or fail the people they serve.

Having personally navigated the realities of incarceration, poverty, fatherhood, and grief, Dr. Shipman brings more than theory—he brings empathy, structure, and proven tools. The Pathway to Renewal (P2R) program was created to offer participants not just recovery, but lasting stability and hope.

WORK WITH DR. KERRY L. SHIPMAN

*"I didn't write this workbook to impress institutions. I wrote it for people who've been counted out.
Healing is messy. Growth takes time. But with structure, support, and the right tools—
we can all rise again."*

— **Dr. Kerry L. Shipman**

Speaking, Consulting & Program Licensing Inquiries

For speaking engagements, program adoption, training, or consulting opportunities, please contact:

Email:

kshipman@Pathway2Renewal.org

Website:

www.Pathway2Renewal.org

National Resources & Lifelines

You've done the inner work. Now here are tools to support your next steps.
These resources can help with mental health, housing, employment, education, crisis response, and staying connected to your recovery and goals. If you need more localized help, speak with your support team—or visit the updated resource list online at:

www.Pathway2Renewal.org/resources

Crisis & Mental Health Hotlines

- **988 Suicide & Crisis Lifeline**
  Call or text **988** anytime — 24/7 confidential support for mental health, suicide, or substance use crises.
  988lifeline.org
- **SAMHSA National Helpline**
  1-800-662-HELP (4357) — Free help for mental health or substance use treatment referrals.
  samhsa.gov/find-help
- **Crisis Text Line**
  Text **HOME** to **741741** — A live, trained crisis counselor will respond 24/7.
  crisistextline.org
- **National Domestic Violence Hotline**
  1-800-799-SAFE (7233) — Support, safety planning, and resources.
  thehotline.org

Housing & Shelter Locators

- **Find Shelter Tool (HUD)**
  Search for low-income housing, emergency shelters, and services.
  findshelter.hud.gov
- **HUD Resource Locator**
  Public housing, housing vouchers, and local providers.
  resources.hud.gov
- **National Coalition for the Homeless**
  Advocacy and directories of local programs.
  nationalhomeless.org

Jobs, Employment & Workforce

- **CareerOneStop**
  A U.S. Dept. of Labor site with job search tools, training, and reentry help.
  careeronestop.org

2025 Pathway to Renewal (P2R) | www.Pathway2Renewal.org | All rights reserved.

- **Indeed**
  The largest job board for local and remote work opportunities.
  indeed.com
- **Apprenticeship Finder**
  Paid training programs by state and trade.
  apprenticeship.gov

Education & GED

- **GED Testing Service**
  Sign up, schedule tests, and get prep support.
  ged.com
- **Khan Academy**
  Free online learning for math, science, reading, and test prep.
  khanacademy.org
- **Coursera / edX**
  Free college-level courses from universities.
  coursera.org / edx.org

Recovery & Peer Support

- **Narcotics Anonymous (NA)**
  na.org
- **Alcoholics Anonymous (AA)**
  aa.org
- **Celebrate Recovery** (Faith-based)
  celebraterecovery.com
- **NAMI (National Alliance on Mental Illness)**
  Peer-led support groups for mental health and families.
  nami.org

Legal & Reentry Support

- **Legal Services Corporation**
  Find free or low-cost legal aid near you.
  lsc.gov
- **National Reentry Resource Center**
  Federal directory for reentry help, jobs, and housing.
  csgjusticecenter.org/nrrc
- **Second Chance Act Resources**
  Programs for people impacted by the justice system.
  nationalreentryresourcecenter.org

Agency Name:_____

Client Acknowledgment & Consent Form

Pathway to Renewal (P2R) Recovery & Stabilization Program

Client Name: _____ **Date of Birth:** _____
Date of Completion: _____
Service Type: ☐ CST ☐ Peer Support ☐ Outpatient Therapy ☐ Other: _____

I, the undersigned, acknowledge, understand, and consent to the following:

1. Client Rights & Responsibilities

I have received information on my rights as a client, including:

- The right to receive services that are respectful, safe, and free from discrimination.
- The right to participate in developing and updating my Person-Centered Plan (PCP).
- The right to accept or decline services.
- The right to have my information kept confidential, except as required by law.
- The right to file a complaint or grievance without fear of retaliation.

2. Participation in the P2R Program & Workbook

I have received the *Pathway to Renewal (P2R)* workbook. I understand:

- The workbook is a recovery and support tool used to guide my progress.
- Completion of workbook activities is voluntary and may be supported by staff.
- It does not replace treatment but supports therapy, case management, and peer services.
- The workbook will be reviewed during planning, team meetings, and discharge.

3. Consent to Receive Services

I voluntarily consent to receive behavioral health treatment and support services, including therapy, case management, peer support, and other clinical interventions as outlined in my Person-Centered Plan through TSG Behavioral Health & Community Services. I understand:

- Services will follow the goals identified in my Person-Centered Plan.
- I may withdraw my consent or request changes at any time.
- I have been oriented to the structure, expectations, and benefits of this program.

4. Crisis Plan Participation & Emergency Resources

I confirm that I:

- Participated in the development of my Crisis & Safety Plan with a provider or staff member.
- Understand the purpose and use of the crisis plan, including how to identify triggers, apply coping strategies, and contact supports.
- Acknowledge receiving a copy of my crisis plan in my workbook.

I have been informed of 24/7 emergency resources available to me if I am in crisis:

- **Mobile Crisis Team:** _____
- **NC Suicide & Crisis Lifeline:** Dial **988**
- **TSG Support Line:** (704) 553-5392

5. Grievance & Complaint Process

I have been informed of my right to file a complaint or grievance about any part of my care. I understand:

- I may file a grievance with TSG staff, my LME/MCO, or directly with NC DHHS.
- Doing so will not affect my services or lead to retaliation.
- I can contact the DHHS Customer Service & Advocacy Office at 1-800-662-7030.

6. Confidentiality & Legal Limitations

I understand that my personal health information will be kept confidential, except in cases where:

- I report thoughts of harming myself or others
- There is suspected abuse, neglect, or exploitation
- A court order or legal requirement demands disclosure

Signatures

Client Acknowledgment

By signing below, I confirm that:

- I have received and reviewed the information in this form
- I understand my rights, consent to services, and acknowledge receiving the P2R workbook and crisis plan
- I have been informed of 24/7 emergency contacts and how to file a complaint

Client Signature: _____ **Date:** _____.
Printed Name: _____

Provider Verification

By signing below, I confirm that:

- I reviewed this workbook and form in full with the client
- I participated in creating the client's Person-Centered Plan and Crisis & Safety Plan
- I reviewed all relevant documentation prior to the start of services
- I oriented the client to the P2R program and answered all questions

Provider Signature: _____**Date:** _____
Printed Name & Credentials: _____.
Title/Role : _____

www.ingramcontent.com/pod-product-compliance
Lightning Source LLC
Chambersburg PA
CBHW062006180426
43198CB00037B/2553